'90s Notebook
Life, Love, & Becoming

a collection of poems

Donna JH Gore

Write On Time Press, LLC
Willingboro, New Jersey

'90s Notebook

Copyright © 2019 Donna JH Gore.

All rights reserved. No part of this publication may be reproduced, distributed, or transmitted in any form or by any means, including photocopying, recording, or other electronic or mechanical methods, without the prior written permission of the publisher.

ISBN: 978-1-7338582-0-5

Library of Congress Control Number: 2019903468

Published by Write On Time Press, LLC (Willingboro, NJ)

Interior Illustrations: Donna JH Gore

Scriptures marked KJV are taken from the KING JAMES VERSION (KJV): KING JAMES VERSION, public domain.

Scriptures marked NKJV are taken from the NEW KING JAMES VERSION (NKJV): Scripture taken from the NEW KING JAMES VERSION®. Copyright© 1982 by Thomas Nelson, Inc. Used by permission. All rights reserved.

Printed in the United States of America

To God, who knows my thoughts before I think them
To Pam, who gave me the notebook to write down my thoughts
To all those who spoke, wrote, sang, danced or breathed something that inspired something in me
I <3 the '90s!

Contents

1: School Days: Black Power! Black Power!

Bittersweet	13
Black Man	14
black secret soul	15
Collage of My Mind's Eye	16
Dear Brothers and Sisters	17
ghetto (urban) IMAGES	18
My Rights Today	19
revolutionary **p**eople	20
What if?	21
Why Do We (Do the Things We Do)?	22
All That is We	23
A Celebration of We	25
Who Do You Think You Are?!	26

2: O, The Children

baby girl	31
man-child	32
No!	33
Gifts as Precious as These…	34
Poverty's Tears	35
Tender Flower	36
WAKE UP! Young Leader	37
When Black Power Met Generation X	38

3: Love Lessons

definitely	43
Desire & The Wall	44
don't leave me (in your heart)	45
Friends for Life	46
God Made You Unique	47
If I could	48
life without you is not life before you	49
not a day	50
they	51
this pen writes so well	52
thoughts for a snowy April day (p.s. i love you)	53
Where I Want to Be	54
Who You Are	55
With You	56
Your (Brown) Eyes	57
When First Love Disappears…	58
[When] A Dove Cries	59
Come Inside	60
Hold Me With Your Heart	61
unspoken words	62
It's a Personal Thang…Understand?	63

4: Think on These Things

Bakari	69
Cloudy Skies	70
A New Day	71
RACISM ends…	72
where was I when…	73

eyes of a child	74
I AM TOO	75
Wendall's Song	76
What Makes a Flower Grow?	78
god of the human mind	79
Windows to the Soul	80
Victory	81
Let Go	82
Life Is	83
Show Love (September 12)	84
Two Were Walking Down the Street	85

5: Saved By Grace

Hallelujah!	91
Happy Birthday	92
Seasons Change	93
I Will Catch You	94
No Introduction to Your Story	95
You Are God's Ability	96
The Brotherhood	97
I Will Return	98
God Help Me	99
When I Am Weak…	100

6: Sanctified Sister

…If I Was a Tree	105
Becoming Statement	106
What Is It You See in Me?	107
Onward Christian Artist	108

7: Nappy Birthday: Liberation 'Me-ology'
    my hair is nappy and i ain't mad   113
    FREEDOM!   114
    independent woman's heart   115

1

School Days: Black Power! Black Power!

She came from a world that was both black and white, nurturing and negating. She entered this new world as a young adult. Eyes open, mind open, she became enlightened by her truths that were once hidden.

'90s Notebook

Bittersweet

Beautiful, smoooth, dark chocolate boy
Ugly, blue-black monkey child

Exotic, mysterious, Mandingo lover
Dumb, sneaky, nigger-boy

Bewildered, misled African man.

Donna JH Gore

Black Man

Black man
Black skin shiny with sweat glistening from the sun's rays sweet like a ripe plum juices flowing after being picked skin peeled away revealing its treasure
Black man
Black hair rough like I like count each kink woven together like wires, brush it, twist it, run fingers through its strength
Black man
Black hands tell your story, with warmth and passion you will hold me, our hands will touch and I will guide you
Black man
Black love—tell me what you're thinking, show me all you are. Speak to me truthfully, choose your words with sincerity…
Black man

black secret soul

an untapped gold mine of intelligence and creativity
do you realize the wealth of your treasure?
unity = strength
vote together
knowledge = power
support one another
power = change
make informed, intelligent choices
release, explore, realize the black secret soul within

inspired by <u>The Autobiography of Malcolm X</u>
-as told to Alex Haley

Donna JH Gore

Collage of My Mind's Eye

Please release me from these chains of bondage—
Not the physical chains my ancestors endured,
But the emotional chains of my being; the stinging pain of the realities of this world.
Feelings of hate, anger, and sadness.
Sections of the past brought to my present like stepping back in time; history repeating itself.
How do we deal with—RACISM? It is all around us.
What do we do with—PARENTS? Raising little white boys and little white girls in little white hoods and little white robes.
What do we do with—INSTITUTIONS? Bent on continuing a tradition of racism.
What do we do with—IDEOLOGIES? That only foster hatred.
What do we do with—PEOPLE? Who refuse to acknowledge injustice.
How do we trust a HIStory that so boldly invades our present?
Oh, I forgot, "We Shall Overcome."
Since Emmet Till and Rodney King, three decades have passed. It's 1992, where have we come?
An explosion erupts inside my brain as fists are clenched and tears roll down my face.
These are my realities. I am a proud black woman. And although that is my strength, I long for some portion of peace in the collage of my mind's eye.

'90s Notebook

Dear Brothers and Sisters

Have you ever known someone who was so intelligent until they seemed ignorant?
Operating like a drunk behind the wheel.
Wake up and see the world in front of you.

Have you ever heard a rapper professing to be so "True to the Game?"
But when the commercial came on, he was rapping with a "40" in his hand?
Selling out to the Almighty Dollar.
Wake up and touch the world you live in.

Have you ever heard brothers just "talkin' that talk?"
Yet every sister is a ho, and every other word is a curse.
Contradicting themselves and confusing others.
Wake up and hear the world around you.

Wake up and taste the power you possess.
Ignorance and intelligence don't mix.

Donna JH Gore

ghetto (urban) IMAGES

sneakers dangle from a telephone wire-a mangy dog roams the street-bullets glide in slow motion-broken glass litters a playground-trash suspended in a field of weeds-boarded-up abandoned buildings-a hydrant flows freely into the street-plastic bags blow from bare trees like leaves-a half-naked baby in diapers stands alone on the sidewalk-plaits are made while sitting on a front stoop-crack vials sprinkle the street like glitter in the sun-grown men lose themselves while drinking from brown paper bags on a corner-spray-painted buildings overwhelm their surroundings-loud music adds to summer's explosion-an innocent victim crosses a stray bullet's path- a woman with soiled clothes pushes her life in a shopping cart-anonymous deals are still made at twilight's insistence-the subway station is heavy with the stench of urine and filth-busy voices occupy busy streets-young girls push strollers by the age of fifteen-the blaring of sirens rises with the sun-profanity drowns out the voices of birds-but we must have hope…if only for flowers in the concrete.

My Rights Today

If I had all my rights today,
What would the amoral majority say?
"Where's MY job, MY house, MY car?
I'VE worked too hard,
WE'VE come too far
To simply stand on equal ground,
Ideals these are,
Not reality bound.
What will be next?
What will they try?
Our spirits kill, then us despise.
No, I fear their wants are too great, and we must keep them in their place.
For when 'our' children go to school,
They'd make them learn of Africa too.
And this is one thing we cannot have,
We brought them out,
They should be glad!"

If I had all my rights today?
Do you know what I would say?
No smile, no "thank you," no "it's about time"—
Just getting from life what was already mine.

Donna JH Gore

revolutionary people

Who put out the fire?
Once thousands of candles burned so bright—
Pure blue,
Strong and steady.
The heat could be felt in D.C. all the way down to Alabama
It was a time that would not be stopped water just seemed to spark other flames giving the fires a boldness that demanded to be fed
The burning scent of wax signaled AIR, AIR, MORE AIR!!
But time caused many wicks to grow dim, some were even snuffed out—before they reached their brightest.
Still, flickering light beckoned to keep hope alive…

Yet the times now are much colder, the road from LA to New York is much darker
No questions are raised,
Quiet is kept.
For there is scarce recollection of a time when fires burned pure and R. P. united.

'90s Notebook

What if?

What if…?
Bronze feet never left their soil,
Planted seeds and watched them grow,
Roots deep, forever strong, entwined as one.
Riches abounding beneath the earth,
Praises given to a promising sky.
They rise to the heights of their intelligence.
They rise to the heights of their being.

What if…?
Bronze feet never left their soil,
No running to find life or oceans overflowing with death,
No labor given freely,
Native jazz,
No ghettos full,
Creativity lost,
No clock ticking away for freedom, truth, justice, and equality.
They live in a world of meaning.
They perish as others soar on.

Donna JH Gore

Why Do We (Do the Things We Do)?

eyes
look away
when you pass me on the street
can't look at me. stand to see yourself?
hey girl, what's up? /look at her think she cute/hey my nigga yo what up? /look at that ho over there what she doin' wit that punk?
high-yellow, half-white, bright-behind, light-skinded, crispy, monkey-lookin', dark-skinded, black dog.
'boom boom boom'
there I go again. dead.
pulled the trigger and there I lay
blood has forged its path in the pavement black
on black on black
black
why do we?

'90s Notebook

All That is We

If a tree is to stand, it must take root deep beneath the soil.
We have forgotten our roots—our anchor, our provider, our strength, our sustainer, our help…

We've forgotten our roots—
Caring, sharing, loving, supporting, working together.
We've forgotten our roots—
Stripped of our dignity; shackles on our ankles.
We've forgotten our roots—
Families divided by an owner's bid.
We've forgotten our roots—
Sting of the whip against our backs.
We've forgotten our roots—
Eatin' the scraps from massah's garbage.
We've forgotten our roots—
Pickin' cotton all day in the hot summer sun.
We've forgotten our roots—
Physical abuses too horrible and numerous to name.
We've forgotten our roots—
Sojourner, Rosa, Harriet.
We've forgotten our roots—
Not allowed to learn how to read and write.
We've forgotten our roots—
Voting was neither a privilege nor a right.
We've forgotten our roots—
Nigger, darkie, Negro, colored, black, African-American.
We've forgotten our roots—
Sitting at the back of the bus.
We've forgotten our roots—
Martin, Malcolm, Marcus, Medgar.
We've forgotten our roots—
Jailed in the struggle for freedom.
We've forgotten our roots—
Shuffling and bowing and smiling, but crying within.
We've forgotten our roots—
Fear and ignorance are wed to produce prejudice, racism, and discrimination.

Donna JH Gore

We've forgotten our roots—
The lynch mob's rope around our necks.
We've forgotten our roots—
Uniting as one to march for our survival.
We've forgotten our roots—
Dogs, water hoses, billy clubs.
We've forgotten our roots—
Killed in the search for truth, justice, and the way.

We've forgotten our roots—
When we can attack Rosa Parks; when we kill one another; when we are apathetic; when we devalue education; when we sell drugs to one another; when we dismiss all that has made us who we are…
When we disrespect, don't look out for, and hurt one another…we've forgotten our roots.

Our beginnings, our source, our Creator, our God.
Not grounded in ourselves.
Not grounded in Him.
We've forgotten our roots—
So how can we stand?

'90s Notebook

A Celebration of We

We are a (*two positive characteristics of our people*) people.
We come from (*description of the continent of Africa*).
We are (*two famous African-American activists*).
(*First line of poem repeated*).

We come in shades of (*three descriptions of our complexions*).
We dream (*something you dream for our people*).
We are (*two famous African-American singers*).
(*First line of poem repeated*).

We have hair that is (*three descriptions of our hair textures*).
We work as (*three positive occupations for African-Americans*).
We are (*two famous African-American writers*).
(*First line of poem repeated*).

We are the inventors of (*two inventions by African-Americans*).
We hope (*something you hope for our people*).
We are (*two famous African-American actors*).
(*First line of poem repeated*).

*input your own text in the parentheses to create a unique poem as an individual or with a group

Donna JH Gore

Who Do You Think You Are?!

Sweat, blood, and tears we shed
To make this nation strong,
Labor freely taken yet you still could hear our song;
"Lift Ev'ry Voice and Sing,"
in Martin's words, "let freedom ring…"
What will it take for unity?
Black, South African mentality?
Cries for justice and equality,
Yet knowledge is not the only key.
Lift your voice, stay informed,
Or the road we have trod
May be lost in the storm.
No longer live in apathy,
Ancestors died for you and me.
Let's make their lives a song of truth,
Get out and vote, there's no excuse.

'90s Notebook

2

O, The Children

Donna JH Gore

'90s Notebook

So sweet and funny. In play and in conversation, she was always drawn to them. She loved the youngest humans. And so, her love grew.

Donna JH Gore

baby girl

sixteen, you thought i was. i could pass.
look older, act older, not one of those giggly girls.
maybe that was the age i gave you?
standing in the schoolyard talking to my friends i could see you out of the corner of my eye.
but you were the one checking me out,
looking at me;
my hair
my body
my face.
you liked what you saw and a part of me that you couldn't see smiled.
but what does this twenty-seven-year-old want with a twelve-year-old?
i know;
even so, i smile.

Donna JH Gore

man-child

little boy
years beyond your life
through your eyes the sad story of generations is told—
rage, abandonment, injustice, ignorance, hostility, indifference, pressures, broken-heartedness, defeat unfold...

in little boys
years beyond your lives
but don't know a thing about living.

'90s Notebook

NO!

How long…
will fires burn untamed?
earth distressed
trembling, screaming, crying—
chaos the heavens never knew
guns, drugs, poverty—
storms of the times.

When will…
the rains cease to fall?
lungs are crushed like a soda can in the path of a speeding train
air is captured for flowers, trees, birds—
now only the rocks can cry out
the cool black sound is a melodic silence.
life's journey reaches its end.

No!
We must plant good seeds in fertile ground.
We must watch our gardens
Our beautiful gardens
We must do better.
We must do better.

Donna JH Gore

Gifts as Precious as These…

Sunrise of a brand-new day
Scent of roses in the air
First fruits of the harvest
Gentle breeze across your face
Birds delightfully singing
But the children—
Oh, the children,
None are gifts as precious as these.

'90s Notebook

Poverty's Tears

Sometimes when I go to bed hungry, cold, dirty...

Face-to-face with the realities of my world—

Rats and roaches searching for crumbs that aren't there.
The McDonald's cashier who can never 'take my order.'
Toys that never existed, but shoes that gratefully did.
The girl scout uniform I can only imagine myself in.
Trips to the candy store that only confirm the cavities in my pockets—

I sometimes wish I would not wake at all...
Or, at least, wake in someone else's dream.

Donna JH Gore

Tender Flower

In time, a young bud will give birth to petals…
But only as life pours into its being
and weeds do not ensnare it.

'90s Notebook

WAKE UP! Young Leader

When I was young my grandma was always fussin' at me;
Pullin' on my clothes, messin' with my hair, checkin' behind my ears, and never lettin' me out of the house for askin' me so many questions.

"Boy, where you goin' with your hair all a mess?
Girl, get in this house, fix your dress.
My yesterday's over,
But you, your time is come
Since time we have wasted
There's work to be done.

"Yeah, we got Jordan, Denzel, TLC, and Shaq
But honey let me tell you we much more than that!
We're Spike, Oprah, and Maya just to name a few
But for the problems of this world, a few just won't do.
We must know math, science, business and such.
Of these things in times past our people knew much.

"Drugs and fighting; having babies before your time?
You destroying your body, you wasting your mind
Not doing your homework?!
Is it fly to act dumb?
While you're in detention
The race can't be run

"In you is the future.
The future is now.
You are Grant Hill, you <u>are</u> Thurgood,
You are Barbara Jordan.
You're Martin, Boyz II Men, and Dr. Ben Carson!

"So, wake up young leader!
What will <u>you</u> do?
'Cause what this world needs—
is you,
you, and YOU!!"

Donna JH Gore

When Black Power Met Generation X

A grandmother asked her grandson,
"What's wrong with the generation of today?
You know, when I was comin' up
Things was not this way.
Folks ain't got no passion,
Can't commit to something for more than a day.
Don't wanna work for nothing,
Just sleep their lives away.
In my time there was caring,
"Hello," "thank you," and "please,"
Love is now perverted like it's some kind of disease.

"Now, to your generation, I'm not trying to complain—
But what is wrong with kids today?
Can you please explain?"

The grandson said to his grandmother,
"You wanna know what's up?
Yeah, You sacrificed, You paid the price,
You 'had a dream,' 'keep hope alive,'
You were the flame, You birthed the sparks
Yet now the times they seem so dark.
So, when I looked in the mirror
It even puzzled me,
Why, in my reflection,
You, I did not see.
My identity is violence, indifference, and fear,
The gap is wide between us,
And my vision isn't clear.
It seems that I don't know you,
And I doubt that you know me,
'Cause when your race you finished running
no one told me where to be.

"So, to your generation,
I'm not trying to lay blame,
But train up a child in the way he should go,
And he won't depart from the same."

'90s Notebook

3

Love Lessons

Donna JH Gore

'90s Notebook

She experienced love, heartache, and false alarms. She found a voice and learned a new language.

Donna JH Gore

definitely

maybe i should not have told you to slow down or rained on your parade maybe you would have come to your own conclusions in your own time maybe i should not have said that we should be apart because now my heart is hurting but maybe we should because your heart is hurting too i know that we both want each other to be happy we want each other to be happy and not sad not crying with head hurting and heart bleeding in pain and confused i know that we care we care deeply i know that i love you

Donna JH Gore

Desire & The Wall

There is a desire in you that longs to be fulfilled. Not the desire for a relationship with God, that you already have. Nonetheless, it is a desire placed in you by God.

A desire for another to enter your world, to touch the place in you that silently cries out to hold a body that is weary, emotions that are complex, a mind that is conflicted, a heart that is sincere, a soul that is fragile, a life that is searching…

Searching for intimacy from behind a brick wall.

A wall—so no one is allowed to enter your world
A wall—so others can't see the places in you that daily cry out
A wall—that when you attempt to dismantle, sends bricks raining down on those who care for you
A wall that forbids outside penetration of a life that is searching, hurting, yearning—

To break free of The Wall of protection that has now become its prison
where it resides alone
with Desire.

don't leave me (in your heart)

If you move to a faraway country, the miles will separate us
Remote places, empty spaces
You're no longer in my reach—
The nearness of you has faded
Your touch a distant memory.

If you forget my picture
The softness of my face
When first you stroked my cheek, my hair
What time has now erased.

If your will to see the good is lost
And the strength of your emotions depleted
Light is dimmed
Hope is lost
Soul's reserves retreated.

When listening to your heart of hearts has become hard to do
The laughter and the joy once heard barely whisper to you
Still deep inside each one, there is a way that points to what is real
That shining star
The one true light
It knows just how you feel.

So, if your mind, your body, soul and strength refuse to do their part
Just promise me one thing you'll do
Don't leave me—
in your heart.

Donna JH Gore

Friends for Life

I don't know where this road's going to lead us
I don't know how our story ends
I don't know what the future has promised
But for now, I'm just glad that we're friends.

I know that God sent you from heaven
I know that this feeling is right
I don't know if we're meant for a lifetime
But I'm having the time of my life.

God Made You Unique

God made you unique
He gave two eyes to see
    yet sometimes through those baby browns, you see things some
    don't see
    but with your eyes you saw me sing
    now you have eyes for me.

God made you unique
He gave two hands to touch
    sometimes things crumble in our hands and seem to turn to dust
    but with your hands you held my hand
    and now I care so much.

God made you unique
He gave a voice to speak
    words can sometimes be unclear, and people disagree
    but with your words I get that burst
    and I'm in ecstasy.

God made you unique
He gave a heart to feel
    sometimes it speaks so softly, its words you cannot hear
    but your heart beats so strong for me
    and now I know how real.

God made you unique

Donna JH Gore

If I could

If I could capture what I feel
I'd create for you a flower
Something new and just for you
To ponder every hour

If I could show you how I feel
I'd just extend my hand
And inside you would find my heart
A love that never ends

'90s Notebook

life without you is not life before you

my life without you would not be like
my life before you.
it would be like being born with sight, then having it taken away,
or smelling the sweetness of a rose for the very last time—
life without you is not life before you.

Donna JH Gore

not a day

not a day goes by that I do not smile.
it's not the sun, skies could be gray,
then thoughts of you they pass my way,
and soon my face gives me away,
your kindness makes me want to say,
whether January or in May,
though time moves on, I'll feel this way,
because of you there's not a day.

'90s Notebook

they

they are new, they are eager, they are scared, they are wanting, they are willing, they have desire, they are learning
they are chris, they are donna, they know love
it is patient, it is kind
if love has anything to do with putting them together, it is hopeful.

Donna JH Gore

this pen writes so well

this pen writes so well.
endless words it wants to tell
soft and loud
on pretty paper
shining in the sun
only for the heart of one.

this pen writes so well.
many stories told
only on paper, written in a book, marked "don't look"
don't see don't listen don't feel
don't
don't look at me like that
don't look into me like that
what do you see?

this pen writes so well.

thoughts for a snowy April day (p.s. i love you)

i've known you for a while, but i want to know you more. just the mere thought of you...in the car, on the job, in my dreams brings me happiness. and yes, the thought of the absence of you brings me pain. even now as that notion enters my mind, a heaviness rests in my heart, and my vision becomes blurry. you are the gentle rain on my window, the path made for me in the night, the smile in my unconscious mind...at times i long to be near you, to see you, to touch you, to stare at you without you knowing i'm there...not a day goes by when i do not smile. yeah, sometimes i cry, but i smile...p.s., i love you.

Donna JH Gore

Where I Want to Be

I imagine that place. It is soft and warm. When I am there, I feel safe; I feel protected; I feel joy. There, I can move around without fear, even do a cartwheel or two. I am content, satisfied; like a baby inside of a mother's womb. I curl up or stretch out in that place. There is a smile on my face…as I listen to the beat of your heart.

'90s Notebook

Who You Are

The beauty of you is beyond what others can see
It surpasses the mere exquisiteness of your external frame
It is what I see when I look straight into your heart
What I see when I stare into your eyes straight to who you are
And you are beautiful
Yes
but with you, beauty is more than skin deep
it is
a matter of the heart.

Donna JH Gore

With You

When I am with you, I feel like I don't want to be without you
I feel happy, content, excited, peaceful...
And when we are near, I want to be closer...to look into your eyes, your mind, your heart.

'90s Notebook

Your (Brown) Eyes

Tell me a story that's all about you,
The world from your point of view.
Communicate what your lips never speak;
What your heart longs to utter.
"What is that you say, look into your eyes?"

Donna JH Gore

When First Love Disappears…

Do birds sing their happy tune?
Or are ears dull to a rejoicing melody?
Does rain fall and meet the earth?
Or is the skin abrasive to the life it gives?
Do colors remain bright and true?
Or do eyes view the world like a watercolor painting?
Is the air still breathable?
Or does the nose only sense the staleness of its surroundings?
Does a kiss taste as sweet?
Or are taste buds numb to desire?
Is the soul open to life?
Or does it hide from the fires of the world?
Does the mind boldly wander?
Or is dreaming a thing of the past?
Does the body speak loudly or whisper?
Or do lifeless emotions abound?
Does the heart soar free and joyous?
Or is it closed when the next love appears?

'90s Notebook

[When] A Dove Cries

From the start, U were like the serpent
And I was the dove.
You said you wanted my heart
But what about love?

The heart is tender, and talk is cheap.
You said you wanted my heart
But did you want me?

Your song was sweet
I melted under your touch.
You stole my heart
But what about us?

Tricks are for kids and games they have rules.
When you play with a heart
Somebody must lose.

From the start, U were like the serpent
And I was the dove.
This is what it sounds like…
Love?

Donna JH Gore

Come Inside

What will you say when you find me in your neighborhood, and I get to your street, and your house is in view...?

   Will you invite me in and tell me to make myself at home?

What will your reaction be when I am close enough to see the things that you've stuffed in the back of your closet, or when the hour is growing late, and I am still sitting in your favorite chair...?

How will you feel when I pretty much know my way around, and I mention that the basement could use a little sweeping?

What will you do when you find yourself in my neighborhood, on my street...?

When I open the door will you come inside?
Breathe the air I breathe?

Will you stand in the hall or take off your shoes?

Do you want to know my journey from the basement to the attic?

   Or would you rather stand on the outside looking in?

'90s Notebook

Hold Me With Your Heart

Hold me with your heart, not your eyes
For the heart knows places eyes will never see

Hold me with your heart, not with words
For the heart speaks of depths that mere words cannot express

Hold me with your heart, not your lips
For the heart ignites the flame and the lips fan the fire

Hold me with your heart, not your hands
For the heart caresses the soul in places hands will never touch

Hold me with your heart.

Donna JH Gore

unspoken words

are the most powerful words…
because they are not words,
but actions
spoken from the heart.

'90s Notebook

It's a Personal Thang…Understand?

If you want a pretty woman to offer a kiss and a kind word…I'm not that woman.

Flattering words and sensitive hands will satisfy a silly woman…but I'm not that woman.

If you want a woman who wants you just because you're a man…I'm not that woman.

"Gimme a man, a job, a car, and a house" …I'm not that woman.

If you want a woman to conform to your fantasies…I'm not that woman.

I
am like no other woman
you have ever known.

I am not THAT woman.

Donna JH Gore

4

Think on These Things

Donna JH Gore

'90s Notebook

Deliberate daydreaming…Her musings on places and times, issues, ideas, and emerging perspectives.

Donna JH Gore

Bakari

The mighty oak is a strong tree.
Tall with branches stretching.
A gust plucked a leaf from its branch, and it fell to the ground.
Day after day it was drowned by the rain and sometimes scorched by the sun.
It became dry and weak, but it did not crumble.
Some days the wind was very strong, and it tossed that old leaf with the force of a hurricane.
But the leaf just drifted from tree to tree.
Never knowing where it came from.
But one spring day that leaf blew so high it could see all the trees beneath it.
And as it drifted along, there was one tree that stood out.
It was a strong tree.
Tall with branches stretching forth, but this tree was bare except for one new bud reaching toward that old leaf.
And as that leaf fell to the ground, it knew this was home. For it crumbled way down into the soil and fed that mighty oak.

Donna JH Gore

Cloudy Skies

I once heard someone say, "Who likes cloudy skies?"
gloomy, cold, dark, dismal, void of sun;
fog rolling, rain approaching,
messy, tiring,
depressing day.

"Who likes cloudy skies?"
Birds still chirping,
Life-giving rain,
Thunder's power,
Skies afire,
Children jumping through puddles,
The aftermath reveals a rainbow,
Lazy, sleepy, thoughtful day,
I like cloudy skies.

'90s Notebook

A New Day

Can you see beyond today?
The many treasures life holds for you.
Your future—like a maze wrapped in shiny, silver paper.
The many different paths you will take, the people you will meet, the places you will see,
Your journey ahead.

Does your mind let you wander beyond four walls?
Taking you to new discoveries,
Envisioning wonderful things to do and experiences to have.

Do your ears let you hear beyond babies crying and sirens blaring?
Does the noise of the world silence your dreams?
Leaving you deaf to sounds you barely heard…
Create a new melody and write it in your heart.
Weather the storms of the world so your song can be heard and never drowned by its waves.

Do your eyes let you see beyond crack vials in the street?
The pain is so strong, your eyes fill with tears blinding your vision.
The gifts you have are lost—to you,
But they can be rebirthed when eyes are made new.

Look beyond today.

Donna JH Gore

RACISM ends...

when truth is the way
when the hating stops
when thinking changes
when the indoctrination ceases
when minds are renewed
when eyes are opened
when paths cross
when lives are touched
when knowledge replaces fear
when ignorance is erased
when tolerance is not equality
when perpetrators stand up for justice
when light pierces darkness
when love is lived.

'90s Notebook

where was I when...

plantations flourishing
America's birth
wars fought
cars rushing
women voting
laws passing
rock rising
students studying
turmoil brewing
people yawning
free love
disco dancing
floppy disks
turmoil approaching
people stretching
turmoil forthcoming
people awakening
turmoil impending
people rising

Donna JH Gore

eyes of a child

Not many grown folks have them;
years of disappointment, greed, betrayal, bitterness—
ofttimes give way to wrinkles and a cloudiness that dulls one's vision.

But I did once see a man who had them—
his curiosity, his individuality, his compassion…
The sparkle in his eyes spoke of optimism and youthfulness;
possibly even innocence or naivete.
Maybe it had something to do with his soul?

I AM TOO

When people say I am
too dark,
too strange, too skinny, too loud,
too proud…

I just smile to MYSELF,
and I say,
"I AM too much!"

Donna JH Gore

Wendall's Song

Where is he going?
What's in all those bags?
Money, a treasure, a lifetime he drags?

Where is his mother,
The giver of life?
Was daddy at home?
Were their days filled with strife?
Was he born a low birth weight?
Did he receive enough love?
Was there food on the table,
And God up above?
Was there space to do homework,
And playtime with friends?
Or was childhood a dream,
When adulthood stepped in?

What is his life like from day to day?
Besides survival is there much else to say?
What is he thinking? Can dreams flash through his mind?
Or is that just a luxury that's since had its time?

What really has happened?
Was this always his life?
Did he sail to far countries?
Make love to his wife?
Did he eat in fine places?
Or study abroad?
Did his job pay the rent?
Were his children adored?

Did society touch him in the least little way?
Did we accept him and shape him or cause him to stray?
How have we failed him?
Or has he failed himself?
Was opportunity there?
Or upon the highest of shelves?

'90s Notebook

Where is he going?
What's in all those bags?
The hope of tomorrow or yesterday's rags?

Donna JH Gore

What Makes A Flower Grow?

What is more important?
The rain or the sun?
The soil or the seed?

The seed makes life a possibility
The soil nurtures life to reality

The sun is light and warmth; urging tender petals to unfold

The rain is wet and refreshing; sustenance for body and soul.

What is more important?
The sun, the rain, the soil, the seed?

The seed without the soil would dry up in its place
Without the rain, the soil would just crumble away
The rain, too, needs the sun to brighten when it's done.

If you ask me what's important,
What makes a flower grow?
The sun, the soil, the rain, the seed
It seems they're all what she needs
To make her grow and to make her strong.

Elements to help her blossom, without them she would die.

Elements to generate her being, without them there would be no life.

god of the human mind

there is a god of the human mind. it is not worshipped. it is anything, yet it is nothing. it conforms to any name around which the mind can be soothed.

tree. star. sun. flower. bird.

But
God is not a tree.
God is not a star.
God is not the sun.
God is not a flower.
God is not a bird.

God is in all these things…and He is God of all.
He commands the leaves to fall, the stars to shine, the sun to rise, the flowers to grow and the birds to fly.

He is the very breath of life, personally initiating a love relationship with man.
So, He asks, how do you love a tree or a star with all your heart, mind, and soul? Can you put your trust in the sun or a flower? Or get direction from a bird?

Look to Me, I am He.

Donna JH Gore

Windows to the Soul

When I looked into her eyes I wanted to cry; not tears of joy, but immense sorrow.
Looking in her eyes, I felt like I was looking through her eyes—
Staring at years of regret
Swallowing miles of bitterness
Enduring utter despair, emptiness, loneliness…unable to visualize true hope.

I never want to look into such sad eyes again
or ever have them gaze back at me when I look in the mirror.

Victory

Hate cannot be understood; it cannot be rationalized or fully explained.

But it can be seen in the eyes of willful men, in hearts that are dark and minds that are oppressed.
With hands and lips, hate is expressed
Likewise, eagerly possessing feet that are quick to mischief, ensnaring the consenting.
Its origins and its symptoms contend for center stage in what is not a game, but a contest nonetheless;
Where the envious, the ignorant, and the fearful shall be defeated, not by might, but by love.

Donna JH Gore

Let Go

Sometimes we want to move ahead, but our mind won't let us.
We see ourselves moving forward; our feet are moving, we are talking, laughing, doing,
Moving, reaching, soaring
Crying, aching
Yearning
To be free
To experience
Being

'90s Notebook

Life Is

They say life is not a destination; it's a journey.
You do not suddenly reach it. One day you don't wake up and obtain it. Life is not to be conquered; it is to be lived. That new house, that new car, the promotion you finally received, your wife and kids…they are not IT. Along your journey they make life enjoyable, but they do not make life.
Jesus said, "I am the way, the truth, and the life…" Make the decision to travel each day with Him and unspeakable joy will be yours for the journey, and your destination will be eternity.

-John 14:6 (KJV)

Show Love (September 12)

September 11, 2001 will forever be etched on our minds. For some, it was the day that they lost their husbands; others lost their jobs or their sons; still others their sense of security. But on September 12, even by noon on September 11, many gained a most precious gift, something that cannot be taken away but is to be given away…freely. That gift, being love, is what Christ showed to us when He died on the cross. It is greater than faith, greater than hope…love never fails! So, believe it, live it, show it.

'90s Notebook

Two Were Walking Down the Street

Two were walking down the street,
One was black, and one was white.
In the city before night,
The one that was black, and the one that was white.
From the sidewalk, eyes were staring,
At the one that was black and the one that was white.
At this couple, hearts were glaring,
Towards the one that was black and the one that was white.
Throughout their journey from the subway station,
Until they reached their destination,
Thoughts unspoken, whispered words,
To the one that was black, were clearly heard.
Was it just imagination?
Sojourner Truth syndrome, agitation?
Maybe a hard day at work?
No caffeine, present hurt?
Or could it have been too much TV?
Too many movies directed by Spike Lee?
Possibly the present reality,
Fostered by this country's history,
So, to the one that was black,
It presented somewhat of a mystery,
For the eyes of the one that was white apparently could not see,
That all along it was more than just
Two walking down the street.

Donna JH Gore

'90s Notebook

5

Saved By Grace

Donna JH Gore

'90s Notebook

A new love, a new awakening; she was reborn!

Donna JH Gore

'90s Notebook

Hallelujah!

As I dreamt in my sleep, You kept me through the night,
You woke me in the morning with the warmth of Your sunlight.
I could walk and talk and hear and smell and taste and see,
And for these many blessings, there is none to thank but Thee.

I looked upon Your earth—Your sky, Your trees, Your creatures great and small,
These things that we call nature—gifts from You each one and all.
I speak to You every day—a friend You are to me,
You calm my fears and hear my prayers – all praises be to Thee.

And even when I do not act as loyal as I should,
You show me over and over again that my God is better than good.
For all the many things You've done and how You've brought me through,
I magnify Your name and give the highest praise to You.

Donna JH Gore

Happy Birthday

In the times that we are living in,
Sometimes it may be hard to see,
All the little lights that shineth,
For the world is filled with grief.

The chaos that the earth survives,
The heavens never knew.
Yet the star the wise men looked upon,
It's in the sky now too.

So now that Christmastime is here,
What we should think of first,
Is the reason why we celebrate,
Jesus Christ's birth.

'90s Notebook

Seasons Change

In winter you came to Me for shelter from the cold. As the winds blew and the snow fell you ran to My love for protection. I held you safely in My arms like a father with a newborn baby.

As spring drew near the earth began to transform. The sun shone life on all it saw. And you began to change in your own way, withdrawing from My side like a child beginning to walk.

By summertime the air had a sweet smell and life was in full bloom. The birds sang, leaves blew, and children played. You too liked to play, running through the field…until you let go of My hand. Then you stumbled, but you still tried to run.

When the leaves began to fall, and the earth closed its eyes you looked for Me. I called your name and heard you crying in the darkness. I opened My arms to embrace My child. For even though the seasons change, My love always remains the same.

Donna JH Gore

I Will Catch You

Trust in Me—
For like the strength of a spider's web,
The gentleness of a single butterfly suspended in a net,
Fireflies playfully guarded inside little hands,
A baby resting on his mother's breast,
The embrace of a father delighting after his child's first steps,
An invisible force lifting you up to where you need to be,
Like a love that fills all space and time,
Safely in the Father's arms—

I will catch you.

No Introduction to Your Story

Foreword by who?
Who was there
but You?
When there was nothing—
but You.
Then You
spoke everything into nothing.
Everything there ever was, is, and is to come.
There is no introduction to Your story.
You are the beginning and the end,
The greatest story ever told;
end of story.

Donna JH Gore

You Are God's Ability

Before the world began,
God had us on His mind,
When He breathed life into humanity
It was all in the fullness of time.
He said, let us make man in our image,
After our likeness, male and female created he,
Flesh and bones are what we are made of,
But who we are, are spiritual beings.
He planted the tree of life from which we could freely eat,
He that eateth my flesh and drinketh my blood, I dwell in him and he in Me.

Through salvation, Christ connects us,
Through prayer, our lives are sustained.
But Christ died for all humanity,
So, for all, we must uphold the banner bloodstained.
By God, we have been given the authority to pray in Jesus' name,
The Holy Spirit gives us power, so that through us, God can reign.

The clash of good and evil is one that cannot be seen,
That is why it must be won by fighting on our knees.
Satan has his army, and he wants us to work for him,
But as children of the light, we bow not to the prince of darkness grim.
We live for the cause of Christ, it is Him we confess and give all glory,
When we come before Him, it is His will we want to free.

But when we say "Amen," the praying doesn't end,
We must always watch and pray,
Listen and obey,
For if God dwells in thee,
You are God's ability.

-John 6:56 (KJV)

'90s Notebook

The Brotherhood

When I see you, I see Jesus—
For in you there is hope.

I see brothers raising holy hands, praising the Lord,
Studying the Word, living for God…

I see providers, protectors, and princes—

So, when they quote their statistics of black men:
In jail, on drugs,
Illiterate, irresponsible, uncaring

I say, "No!"
For there – is hope.

Donna JH Gore

I Will Return

The Lord He tested Abraham
For he had to be proved.
God said, take your only son
Go where I tell you to.

When you get to the place I say
Isaac you will take,
Lay him on the altar
And offer him there for My sake.

So, Abraham rose up early
With his son and others, he did sojourn.
When he lifted his eyes and saw the place
He told them, stay here, the boy and I will return.

How could Abraham say this?
Because he was strong in faith.
He staggered not at the promise of God
Knowing the Lord had made a way.

He against hope believed in hope,
And being persuaded that He who promised was able to perform,
Was imputed to him for righteousness,
Though not for his sake alone.

For if we believe as Abraham,
In the One who with us ever sojourns,
When tests and trials come our way,
We too will know that we shall return.

-Genesis 22 & Romans 4:18-24 (KJV)

God Help Me

This plea gets results, not because it is a plea of desperation of the right combination to a magic formula…
It works because it is a prayer of a sincere heart that knows it needs God.
It works because the One to whom the statement is directed hears, listens, and answers.
And so, it is stated in His Word, "call to Me and I will answer you…"

-Jeremiah 33:3 (NKJV)

Donna JH Gore

When I Am Weak…

It is true that life can deliver blows with the force of a speeding train; knocking us off of our high horses, shaking us loose of our dependence on self, changing our perspective on what it is we hold dear—things we once prided ourselves in, showing us how weak we really are. But, isn't it wonderful to know that God doesn't allow circumstances to show us how weak we are? It is not His desire to leave us mulling over our inadequacies, failures, and setbacks. He wants not only to pour into us, but to release through us. Yes, thank God, it is also true that in our inevitable times of weakness, He is the strength on whom we can depend.

6

Sanctified Sister

Donna JH Gore

'90s Notebook

Where would this new love take her? How would it shape her? She was a woman growing in newness.

Donna JH Gore

...If I Was a Tree

If I was a tree my branches would be long, reaching, stretching...
Because of all the life that has been poured into me.
...if I was a tree.

My buds would burst into leaves
Joyfully swaying in His breeze,
...if I was a tree.

My roots, they'd dig beneath the earth,
Life-giving soil that gave me birth,
I'd wish all trees could be like me, that is...
If I was a tree.

But since I was not made a tree,
I praise Him for the miracle of me!

Because just like that tree I am growing in His love,
My joy is overflowing since He chose me from above.
My faith is firmly rooted in Jesus Christ the Son,
The new life that He gave to me,
I want for everyone!

Everything that is, He made it,
Including you and me.
So, don't let anything steal your praise for Him,
Even that old tree.

Donna JH Gore

Becoming Statement

Prepare me to be the person I am...

The one You created
before I was.

'90s Notebook

What Is It You See in Me?

What is it you see in me?
What something caught your eye?
A pretty smile, a bashful laugh,
Perhaps a soft reply.

> Well, I am like a diamond
> Hidden from most eyes,
> People cannot see my wealth
> With just the naked eye.

What do you think about me?
When I pass your way?
Lingering perfume or the motion in my sway.

> See, I am like a star
> Twinkling in the night.
> The pure and precious gift
> Of God's redeeming light.

What is it you want from me?
Is it something I possess?
The virtues of my womanhood
Much more than just a kiss.

> But, I am like a flower,
> Firmly planted in good ground.
> Waiting patiently on Him
> Till my time to bloom is found.

Donna JH Gore

Onward Christian Artist

Yes, I am a Christian artist.
And it does not offend me when you label me as such;
Doesn't box me in,
No, it sets me free.

7

Nappy Birthday: Liberation 'Me-ology'

Donna JH Gore

'90s Notebook

Digging deeper into who she was, her roots began to tell her story.

Donna JH Gore

'90s Notebook

my hair is nappy and i ain't mad

my hair is nappy and i ain't mad
though you may see me and shake your head
to me, what i've got isn't 'bad'
my natural hair is not a fad
it's just the way that my hair grows
and so i let it
now you know
whether frizzy, curly or kinky
these tresses stresses to be free!

Donna JH Gore

FREEDOM!

Freedom!
From this black woman's perspective—
Just say no
to the collective
way of thinking.
Fried, dyed, laid to the side,
Saturday all day beauty foray…
No way.
I say,
I just gotta be me.
Naturally.
Walkin' in the rain, ain't no thang,
Clouds hang low, let it snow,
Hu-mid-i-ty's all right with me.
See, people talk about keepin' it real
But everybody can't feel me
Free
From restrictions
Black, white or otherwise.
It took a while,
But my style and my convictions cry…
FREEDOM!!

'90s Notebook

independent woman's heart

before us
i want to feel me
move in my own space
look at my toilet seat
down

www.ingramcontent.com/pod-product-compliance
Lightning Source LLC
LaVergne TN
LVHW011210080426
835508LV00007B/706